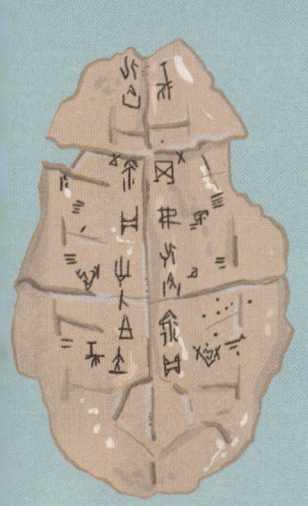

WHAT WOULD YOU BE?
in Ancient China

First published in Great Britain in 2024
by NQ Publishers, an imprint of Nextquisite Ltd.

Copyright © 2024 by Nextquisite Ltd

All rights reserved. Unauthorised reproduction,
in any manner, is prohibited.

www.nqpublishers.com

www.nextquisite.com

Project Director Anne McRae
Art Director Marco Nardi

Illustrations Steph Marshall
Text Mary Auld
Editing Rachel Cooke and Andrew Cornwell
Picture Research Nicola Burns
Graphic Design Marco Nardi
Layout Design Jeni Child

ISBN 978-1-912944-60-6

Printed in China

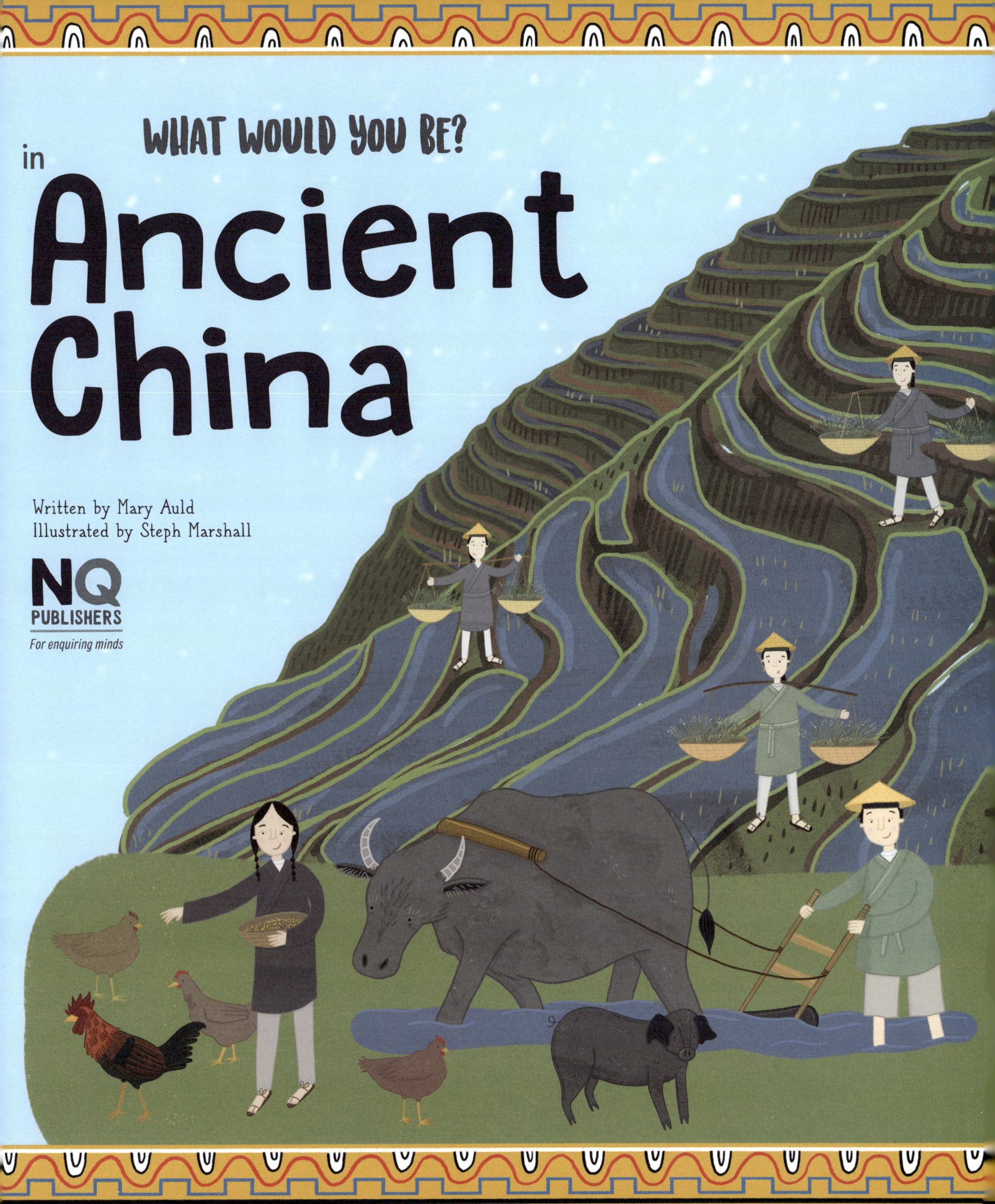

CONTENTS

LIVING IN ANCIENT CHINA   10
Introduction / Timeline

THE YOUNG FARMERS   12
Farming and Food

THE YOUNG EMPEROR   14
Ruling China

WOMEN OF THE PALACE   16
Life at Court

CHENG'S BIG EXAM   18
Exams and Administration

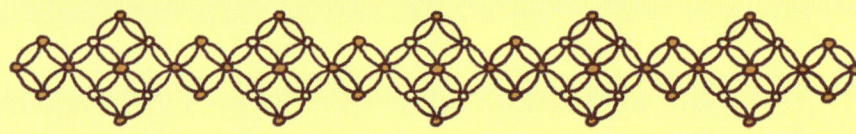

THE BOY WARRIOR   20
Warfare and Weapons

THE SILK MAKER'S DAUGHTER   22
The Importance of Silk

THE PAPERMAKER'S SON   24
Paper and Printing

THE TIMEKEEPER'S DAUGHTER   26
Calendar and Time

THE ALCHEMIST'S CHILDREN Technology and Inventions	28
THE TRAINEE DOCTOR Medicine and Science	30
THE YOUNG POET Poetry and Literature	32
THE PEAR GARDEN Music and Entertainment	34
BANDITS ON THE SILK ROAD Merchants and Trade	36

THE YOUNG MONK Religion and Beliefs	38
THE MATCHMAKER'S ASSISTANT Marriage and Daily Life	40
QUIZ TIME!	42
INDEX	44

Dates in this book are shown as BCE (Before Common Era) and CE (Common Era). The Common Era starts with year 1.

TIMELINE

BEFORE THE EMPIRE
(8000–3000 BCE)
From early farming settlements, small, separate kingdoms form led by the first named emperors and dynasties.

THE QIN DYNASTY
(221–206 BCE)
China united for the first time. Writing system standardised and the Great Wall of China built.

THE HAN DYNASTY
(206 BCE–220 CE)
A strong civil service established. Many technological advances made. Silk Road is open across Asia.

SIX DYNASTIES PERIOD FOLLOWED BY SUI DYNASTY
(220–618)
Buddhism now widespread.

THE TANG DYNASTY AND FIVE DYNASTIES PERIOD
(618–960)
Art and culture blossom under the Tang. Strong international trade. Five dynasties period begins in 907.

THE SONG AND YUAN DYNASTIES
(960–1368)
The Song strengthen education and broaden entry to the civil service. Mongols invade and form the Yuan dynasty in 1271.

THE MING DYNASTY
(1368–1644)
The Ming push out the Mongols. Sea trade becomes more important, leading to direct contact with Europe.

THE QING DYNASTY
(1644–1912)
China's last imperial dynasty, run in a similar way to the Ming. Imperial power declines and China becomes a republic.

479 BCE

The death of Confucius
China had developed a writing system by 1000 BCE. This meant that the ideas of the great philosopher Confucius were written down and studied for centuries after his death.

125 CE

Zhang Heng makes an invention
A civil servant and scientist, Zhang Heng designs a water-powered armillary sphere to follow the stars and planets in the sky. This is one of many technological innovations in the Han era. Another was papermaking.

1420 CE

The Forbidden City is built
Built under the Ming dynasty, this massive palace complex in Beijing becomes China's centre of government until the last emperor resigns in 1912.

214 BCE

Construction of the Great Wall
The first emperor of a united China, Qin Shi Huang, orders that the various defensive walls in North China should be joined together. This becomes the Great Wall of China.

700s CE

The Pear Garden Academy is opened
The Tang emperor Xuanzong (ruled 712–756 CE) founds a school for the performing arts in his capital city. The Tang era is often described as a Chinese 'Golden Age' for the creative arts.

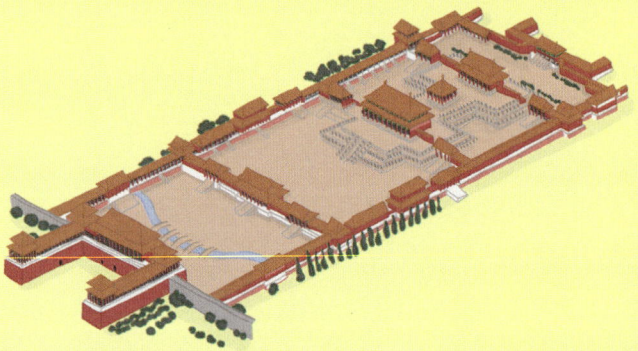

LIVING IN ANCIENT CHINA

Let's travel back in time some 2,250 years to when China was united for the first time. We will find a new country already rich in tradition. Farmers have learnt to flood paddy fields to grow rice, women have woven incredible silk cloth and great philosophers have written important guides to life. We will see these traditions continue as we travel through ancient China's imperial age of dynasties and emperors that lasted to the 20th century. Yet amongst these traditions there are also many changes and innovations. We will meet Tao and Yu Yan, the alchemist's children, and see the invention of gunpowder! There's Chao, a papermaker's son, who knows all about printing. We'll spend time with Baozhai, a talented poet who writes with beautiful calligraphy. And we will meet many more: a young princess, a hardworking student, a soldier stationed on the Great Wall, a silk maker's daughter and boys travelling the Silk Road. We will even visit one of the first schools for the performing arts and tumble with the acrobats in front of the Emperor!

THE YOUNG FARMERS

Most people in ancient China were poor farmers. They lived in villages and looked after small plots of land. They did not own the land, which usually belonged to a local noble family. At times, farmers had to help their rulers by fighting in the army and working on big building projects, such as the Great Wall.

FARMING IN CHINA

The origins of farming
Farming in China began along its great rivers. Farmers in the north grew millet by the Yellow River. Those in the south cultivated rice along the Yangtze. This early farming culture led to the development of China's civilisation.

JUNJIE

Hi, I'm Junjie. I'm 12. I work with my family on our farm. I have lots of ideas for new crops but my dad doesn't always agree!

PING

Junjie and Ping get up early every day.

Junjie uses a wheelbarrow to move heavy loads around the farm.

A hand cart
The wheelbarrow was invented in China more than 2,000 years ago.

Hello, I'm Ping, Junjie's little sister. I'm only nine but I work on the farm too. I take care of the hens and other animals.

Farm animals
Farmers owned chickens and pigs and sometimes an ox or a mule for transport or ploughing. Most of the work was done by hand.

Hens

Pigs

An ox pulls Junjie's plough through the paddy field. The Chinese were the first to use an iron ploughshare.

This iron plough really cuts through the mud!

Crops
Rice and millet gave the Chinese their main food but farmers grew other crops too. These included tea, sugar and cotton. In the 16th century new crops such as sweet potatoes, maize and peanuts were introduced to China from other parts of the world.

Ploughing took place in the spring, weeding in the summer and harvesting in autumn. Food was stored for the winter.

RICE TERRACES
In hilly areas, rice farmers built terraces into the hillsides. It was a lot of work. They chose slopes with plenty of water and with building materials nearby, such as stones and topsoil. Well-built rice terraces lasted for hundreds of years, but they needed to be carefully looked after. The rice had to be planted and harvested by hand. You can still see these amazing terraces in parts of China today.

Rice farming
Over 7,000 years ago, the Chinese discovered that the rice grew better in flooded fields than in dry ones. This way of growing rice in paddy fields continues to this day.

Ping goes with her mother and aunts to plant rice in the paddy fields. It is back-breaking work!

These baskets are heavy!

THE YOUNG EMPEROR

China was ruled by emperors for over 2,000 years. An emperor was known as the 'Son of Heaven'. The first emperor to rule a united China came to power in 221 BCE. The last emperor resigned in 1912 CE. Emperors were the head of a royal family, or dynasty, and most inherited their role – but not always. There were a lot of battles for power. Sometimes boys like Zhao became emperors. They ruled with the support of an adult, often their mother, until they were old enough to rule for themselves.

Hello, I'm Zhao. I'm Emperor of all China – but I'm only ten! It's hard work leading a dynasty!

ZHAO

A DAY IN THE LIFE OF A CHINESE EMPEROR

The emperors had busy lives with many official duties to perform, but they also had some time for themselves.

4 a.m. The Emperor takes requests surrounded by his advisers. People bow low or 'kowtow' before him when they ask for his help.

9 a.m. The Emperor studies. As a religious leader and 'Son of Heaven', he was expected to work hard and know a great deal.

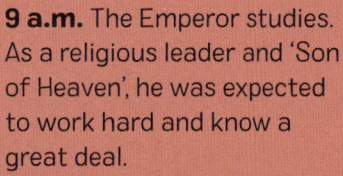

This book is difficult!

Oops, missed again!

1 p.m. The Emperor relaxes. He had leisure time: hunting, drinking tea or sitting in the garden with one of his many wives, or concubines.

4 p.m. The Emperor sets out on tour. As the leader of such a huge empire, he was expected to travel around China to see his people.

A leader of religion

As the 'Son of Heaven', the Emperor was the representative of heaven on Earth. He carried out many religious duties, including making sacrifices and saying prayers at specially built temples. The ceremonies were for the well-being of his people, for example asking for a good harvest.

After a ceremony inside the temple, the Emperor blessed the people waiting outside.

The Temple of Heaven in Beijing was built at the same time as the Forbidden City.

Great palaces

The Emperor ruled from a great palace, surrounded by his family, court and administrators. From 1420 CE onwards, this palace was the Forbidden City – a huge complex built in the centre of Beijing, which had just become China's capital city under the new Ming dynasty. It had 980 buildings with over 8,500 rooms. At one point, as many as 9,000 people lived there.

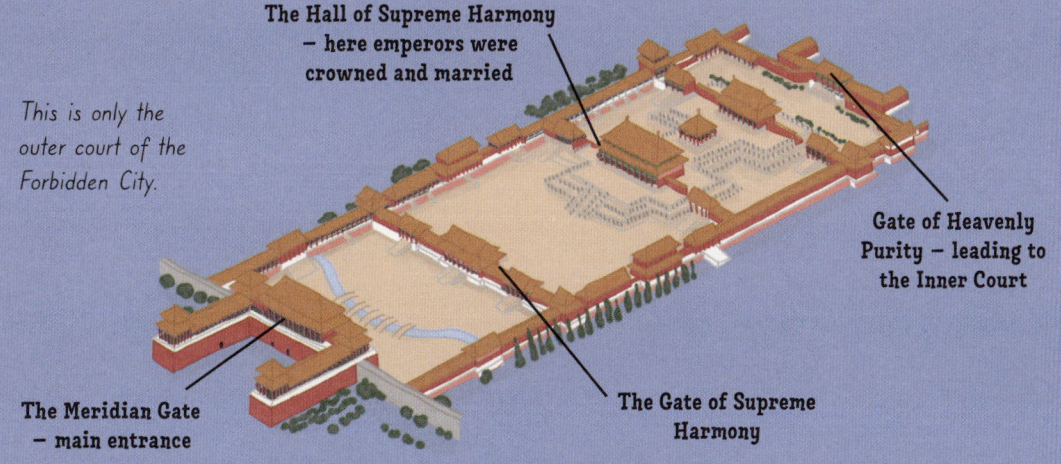

This is only the outer court of the Forbidden City.

- The Hall of Supreme Harmony – here emperors were crowned and married
- Gate of Heavenly Purity – leading to the Inner Court
- The Meridian Gate – main entrance
- The Gate of Supreme Harmony

GREAT EMPERORS

There were more than 550 Chinese emperors and 83 different dynasties. Here are just three of them.

Qin Shi Huang (ruled 221–210 BCE) was China's first emperor. He built the first Great Wall of China and was famously buried with a clay (terracotta) army.

Kublai Khan (ruled 1271–1294 CE), grandson of Ghengis Khan, was a Mongol leader who conquered China and founded the Yuan dynasty (1271–1368).

Qianlong (ruled 1735–1796) was part of the Qing dynasty. During his long reign, he greatly expanded the lands controlled by China.

WOMEN OF THE PALACE

PRINCESS KUNYI

I'm Princess Kunyi. I'm part of the royal family. Ming Yue is my servant but we like to play together.

Hello, I'm Ming Yue (that means Bright Moon). I am a palace maid. I was specially chosen to work here.

MING YUE

Many women lived in the imperial palace. Leading them all were the Emperor's wife (the Empress) and his mother (the Dowager Empress). Then came his daughters, royal princesses like Kunyi. Some women courtiers helped run the palace. Alongside them were many servants, like Ming Yue, and craftworkers. The Emperor also had many concubines, lower-level wives, chosen to have sons with him to carry on the dynasty.

The inner palace

The women of the royal palace rarely left the inner court. Each member of the royal family had her own maids and companions. She might even have her own female doctor. These servants were often chosen for her by the Dowager Empress.

It's important for the Empress to have the best make-up.

Maids at the palace were often skilled in crafts. They would make cloth and clothes, as well as food and medicine. Some made make-up for the women of the court.

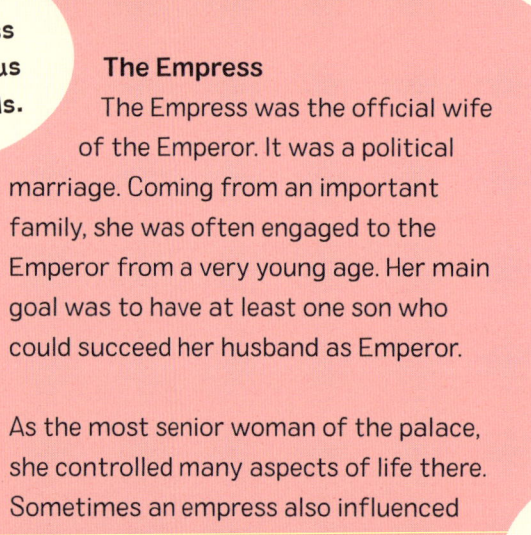

Do you like my rosy cheeks and cherry lips?

Princess Kunyi and Ming Yue like to experiment with make-up!

I'm pleased with the flower pattern over my nose.

You can tell I'm the Empress from my fabulous clothes and jewels.

The Empress

The Empress was the official wife of the Emperor. It was a political marriage. Coming from an important family, she was often engaged to the Emperor from a very young age. Her main goal was to have at least one son who could succeed her husband as Emperor.

As the most senior woman of the palace, she controlled many aspects of life there. Sometimes an empress also influenced her husband. More importantly, she influenced her son when he became Emperor and she the Dowager Empress.

THE EMPRESS WU

Wu Zetian (ruled 690–705 CE) of the Tang dynasty was the only female emperor in Chinese history. She was officially emperor for the last 15 years of her life, but she was the real ruler long before that. Wu began her career as a concubine, but she was the Emperor Gaozong's favourite. She also had several sons by him, while his official wife had none.

Wu ruthlessly used her influence over the Emperor to take on power. Gaozong made her Empress Consort in 655. She was a clever politician and ruler. During her reign, China greatly expanded its empire and its arts and culture blossomed.

The jade Heirloom Seal of the Realm was used from the time of the first emperor to approve official documents. The Empress Wu used it too, calling it 'a treasure'.

The concubines

The secondary wives, or concubines, of the Emperor were chosen from all over China. Young women were selected for their beauty and health, so they would have healthy children. The Emperor was expected to have many children, in particular sons. With several hundred concubines at one time, some rarely saw the Emperor. They spent much of their time with the other concubines and women of the palace.

The way concubines dressed could tell you their status.

Maids waited on them and kept them cool with fans.

"Good move!"

"Did you hear who is with the Emperor today?"

Women chatted, sewed and read.

The women painted each other's faces and created elaborate hairstyles.

Some played games, like this strategy game called 'Go'.

Footbinding

During the Song dynasty (960–1279 CE), people began binding girls' feet, breaking them, then wrapping them in bandages to keep them small. Most of the women of the palace had bound feet. Footbinding was thought beautiful, but it gave women great pain and made it hard for them to walk. It was made illegal in the 20th century.

Women wore tiny slippers over their bound feet.

CHENG'S BIG EXAM

To control and keep a huge country like China running smoothly, the emperors developed a large civil service of government administrators. From the 7th century, the men who worked for this were chosen by difficult, competitive exams. They were known as scholar-officials.

Open to all
The civil service exams were originally only taken by people who came from noble families. Later on, though, boys from poorer families, like Cheng, could take the exam, giving them the chance to move up the social ladder.

Grouping the people
Below the Royal Family, the Chinese were put into four groups depending on what they did. Some types of worker and slaves were placed outside these. It was hard to move between the groups.

SHI
Scholar-officials mainly made up this group but it also included army generals and the land-owning nobility.

NONG
Farmers made up this group. They were important as they provided food.

GONG
Craft workers and artisans made up this group, including stonemasons and silk makers.

SHANG
Merchants and traders made up this group. Often wealthy, some also acted as moneylenders.

Chinese schools
Schools existed from very ancient times. Many were run by the government. Only boys attended. They learnt to read and write (including calligraphy, where writing is treated as a form of art), as well as maths. They studied poetry, music and history.

The ideals of Confucius
One important part of their studies was the writings of Confucius, a very important Chinese thinker (see page 39). His ideas helped form the methods and systems of the Chinese civil service.

Cheng is keen in class.

ON TO COLLEGE

As part of the training for the civil service, older boys went on to university, first at a local level and then at the Imperial College in the Chinese capital. A student had to study here to qualify to become the highest level of official, passing exams called 'jinshi'. Studies centred around classical Chinese writing, dating back to before the first emperor. These included the works of Confucius.

The Beijing Guozijian was first built during the Yuan dynasty to be its Imperial College. The Emperor would go there to read from the Chinese classics to the students.

The life of a scholar-official

Once you had passed the exams to become a scholar-official, you had a very busy job, working ten days in a row starting at 5 a.m. Responsibilities could include trade and finance, law and justice, and making sure the country ran smoothly both at national and regional levels.

> When will the bright moon light my journey home?

WANG ANSHI

The Chinese character for water is often linked to Confucius. It symbolises 'the source of life'.

Poets and philosophers

Scholar-officials were not only trained in administration but were also very knowledgeable about poetry and philosophy (following the ideals of Confucius). Many were respected as poets and thinkers in their own right, such as Wang Anshi (1021–1086) who worked during the Song dynasty. He also undertook major administrative reforms.

Wealth and privilege

Scholar-officials were well-paid and well-looked after. They were entertained at lavish banquets several times a week and had many privileges. Their wealth allowed their families to have luxurious homes. A scholar-official might have concubines and also his own personal entertainers, musicians and dancers.

The exam

After passing exams at several different levels and studying at the Imperial College, students like Cheng were ready to take the *jinshi* exam. They gave their written papers to the official examiner, bowing low as a mark of respect. At some times in history, the Emperor would set the exam and interview the candidates himself.

A successful candidate not only had a job for life but he could now wear the robes of a scholar-official, decorated with birds.

> May I present Cheng as a candidate?

> I have written my essay in the correct way.

THE BOY WARRIOR

From very early on, the Chinese had built walls to defend their land from raids by northern tribes. The first emperor, Qin Shi Huang, joined up these walls to form the Great Wall of China. Later dynasties carried on his work. The Ming dynasty (1368–1644) added spectacular forts and watchtowers.

Greetings! I'm Zihao, I'm 14 but already a soldier on the Great Wall. China is under attack!

ZIHAO

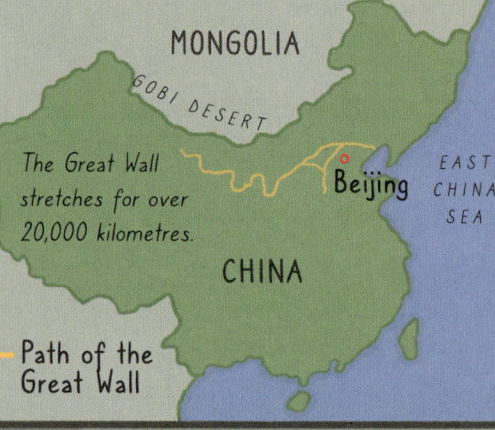

The Great Wall stretches for over 20,000 kilometres.

— Path of the Great Wall

Building the Great Wall
The Wall was never one single structure. Different dynasties built different parts or improved existing defences. Soldiers, slaves, convicts and local labourers did the back-breaking work. The Great Wall snaked over hills and plains from the Gobi Desert to the East China Sea.

The stone outer walls were filled with earth and rubble for strength.

A soldier's life
The army patrolled and lived along the Great Wall. Soldiers' sons became soldiers too. Young men like Zihao helped maintain the Wall. They were ready to light warning fires when under attack.

They'll never get through our defences.

Pass guards

Soldiers on patrol

A pass

Gate

Halt! Who goes there?

Passes were heavily-protected forts and gates within the wall. Soldiers lived here, controlling who came through the gate.

THE NAVY
As well as an army, the Chinese had a navy from as early as the Han dynasty (206 BCE–220 CE). Ships patrolled the rivers and were used to protect sea shipping and trade. The Chinese developed a 'castle' ship – a floating fortress, full of men and heavily armed.

Castle ships were rowed into battle along the River Yangtze.

Crenellated walls

Beacons

Soldiers lit fires in the watchtowers to communicate along the wall.

Watchtower

The Mongols were fierce warriors, famous for fast attacks on horseback.

Mongol cavalry attack

"Keep those beacons burning."

The Wall was so wide that as many as four horses could ride side-by-side along it.

The Mongols

From the 13th century, one of the main threats to China were the Mongol tribes. Led by Genghis Khan, their armies managed to break through the Wall several times. The Mongols eventually conquered China and founded the Yuan dynasty.

The Ming dynasty pushed out the Mongols in 1368. The Ming rulers reinforced the Great Wall to protect their lands, but the Mongols attacked again several times, even capturing the Ming emperor.

A chariot gave a commander a good view of the battlefield.

WEAPONS OF WAR

The Chinese developed many weapons, in addition to bows and arrows, swords and spears. Chariots were good for fast attacks but also could make defensive lines. There were chariots among the first emperor's terracotta army (see page 15) but their use died out after this. In the 9th century, the Chinese invented gunpowder. This led to the development of the first canons, bombs and rockets.

Fire arrows were the first weapons to use gunpowder. They were launched from hand-held baskets.

HOW SILK WAS INVENTED

There are many legends about how silk was invented. This one is famous: A long time ago, the Empress Leizu, wife of the legendary Yellow Emperor, was sitting beneath the mulberry trees in her garden drinking tea when the cocoon of a silkworm fell into her cup. As she took it out, it unravelled as a thread. Leizu wove it into a fabric of astonishing beauty. She showed her courtiers how to make the fabric, and she later became known as the goddess of silk.

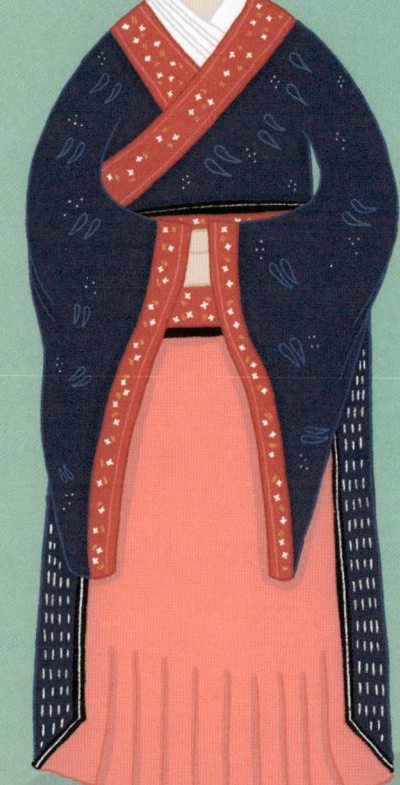

As the Emperor's favourite, I only wear the finest silk robes.

Silk clothes and other uses

Silk clothes were a status symbol as only wealthy people could afford them. Often the clothes were embroidered with complex designs of flowers and birds. Merchants and peasants were only allowed to wear silk from the 17th century.

Silk was also used to make other things, such as paper, strings for musical instruments, and a basis for paintings.

Shan's aunt spins the threads from the cocoons into a single, strong thread ready for weaving.

A trader was asking me about silk making. Of course, I didn't say a word...

Spinning wheel

Spindle

Loom

Shan's mother completes the job by dying the thread and weaving it into a fabric on a loom.

A well-kept secret

The Chinese kept the silk-making process secret for hundreds of years so that foreigners were forced to buy the expensive cloth from Chinese merchants. Anyone caught smuggling silkworms out of China was put to death. But around 1,500 years ago the secret was out and silk was soon being made in many parts of Asia and Europe.

THE PAPERMAKER'S SON

Hello, I'm Chao. I'm 10. My family are papermakers. I love to watch them work. I help out sometimes, too.

CHAO

The Chinese started making paper during the Han dynasty. They used a mix of rags and plant fibres. With all their official documents, paper quickly caught on. The Chinese papermaking industry grew fast. It needed a large workforce, including the help of young boys like Chao.

Uses for paper
Paper was used for writing, painting and, of course, creating books. At first, these took the form of scrolls. Paper had many other uses, from military maps to packaging for tea and medicine. When stiffened, it could also be used for armour and window coverings.

Paper hats gave outdoor workers excellent protection from the sun.

HOW PAPER WAS MADE

The materials used for making paper changed over time, but long fibres were always needed to help mesh the paper together. High quality paper used different ingredients than cheaper types.

1. Bamboo was often used to make paper. It was easy to grow and harvest.

Be careful. Don't splash!

2. The chopped-up bamboo was soaked in lime to clean and soften it.

3. It was boiled so the bamboo broke up and its fibres separated.

4. The bamboo mix was beaten to a pulp.

5. A screen was dipped into the pulp. A layer of pulp formed on the screen.

Don't get any fingerprints on the paper.

6. This was pressed and dried to create a finished sheet of paper.

Woodblock printing

Around 700 CE, the Tang Chinese developed woodblock printing. Chinese characters (their system of writing) were carved in reverse onto a wooden block, which was covered with black ink and then printed onto a paper sheet so it could be read the correct way round. Printing allowed scroll and then book production to boom. Many more Chinese learnt to read and write.

Moveable type

Several different Chinese inventors, such as Wang Zhen in the 13th century, developed moveable type printing. Separate character blocks were made up into pages to print from. Perhaps because there were so many Chinese characters (over 30,000), woodblock printing remained popular.

I wonder if this moveable type will catch on?

To hold his moveable type, Wang Zhen developed rotating frames. These made a character easier to find when creating pages.

Moveable type characters were carved into wooden blocks like these. Later they were cast in metal from moulds. They could be reorganised and reused many times.

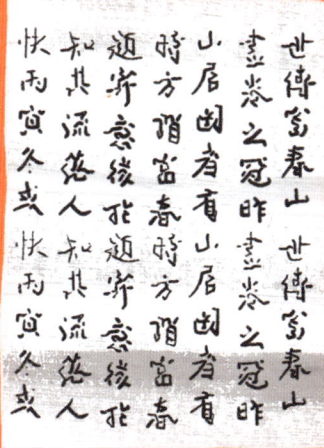 

A printed page of Chinese characters and the woodblock (carved in reverse) that it was printed from.

Chinese innovation

Like silk, Chinese paper was greatly prized and they exported it around Asia and eventually to Europe. They tried to keep how it was made a secret, too, but the knowledge gradually leaked out. The Chinese were the first people known to use woodblock printing and this technology too spread around Asia. Moveable type was first used in Europe in the 15th century.

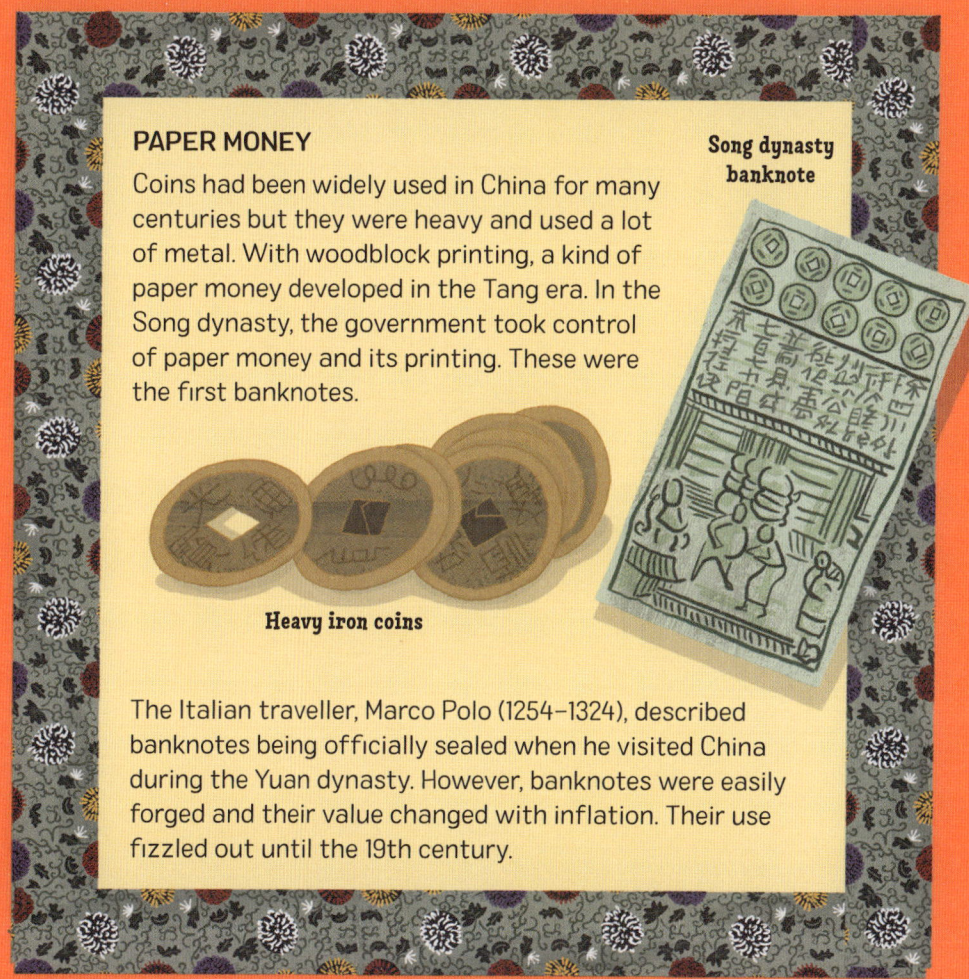

PAPER MONEY

Coins had been widely used in China for many centuries but they were heavy and used a lot of metal. With woodblock printing, a kind of paper money developed in the Tang era. In the Song dynasty, the government took control of paper money and its printing. These were the first banknotes.

Song dynasty banknote

Heavy iron coins

The Italian traveller, Marco Polo (1254–1324), described banknotes being officially sealed when he visited China during the Yuan dynasty. However, banknotes were easily forged and their value changed with inflation. Their use fizzled out until the 19th century.

THE TIMEKEEPER'S DAUGHTER

The ancient Chinese measured time differently than today. A year was measured by the position of the sun and the changing size of the moon. The day was divided into 12 'shi'. Timekeepers like Ah Lam's father hit bells or drums to mark the passing of time through the day and night.

AH LAM

Hello, I'm Ah Lam. I've just turned six and I'm learning how to tell the time from my dad — he lets people know the time.

Years and months
A year was measured by the position of the sun in the sky and the changing shape (phases) of the moon. A new year usually began on the second new moon (when the moon is not visible) after the winter solstice (the shortest day of the year). The Chinese year usually had 12 months, again linked to the moon's phases. About every three years an extra month was added to keep a year linked to the winter solstice.

Dividing the day
What we know as the 24 hours of the day, the Chinese divided into 12 shi, two-hour intervals which were given names such as 'sunset' or 'dinner time'. In addition to this, there was a smaller measure of time called a 'ke', which divided the day into a hundred. By combining the two, it was possible to give very accurate time checks.

Water clocks like this Han dynasty one were found throughout the Empire's civil service so that official documents could be dated and timed.

Each year is linked to one of the 12 animals of the Chinese Zodiac. The Chinese believe animals of their Zodiac bring certain qualities to the year they are linked with and to the people born that year.

Measuring the time

To measure the passing time, the Chinese developed various machines. Sundials showed the time by the position of the shadow cast by the sun but these did not work at night. From very early on the Chinese used water clocks, where the amount of water that dripped from a container at a steady speed was measured to mark the passing hours. During the Han dynasty, water was also used to turn an armillary sphere, a device to help calculate the date (see page 31).

A sundial's markings were divided to show the different measures of time the Chinese used..

Hmmm. The sun has set. I think it is my bedtime.

SU SONG'S COSMIC ENGINE

Su Song (1020–1101) was a scholar-official but also a great scientist and engineer. He is most famous for his astronomical clock tower completed by 1094. Powered by a water wheel, it stood over 12 metres high and used a system of wheels and cogs to tell the time. An armillary sphere linked to a celestial globe also turned to show the movement of the stars. Mechanical figures rang bells and held up signs to show the hour.

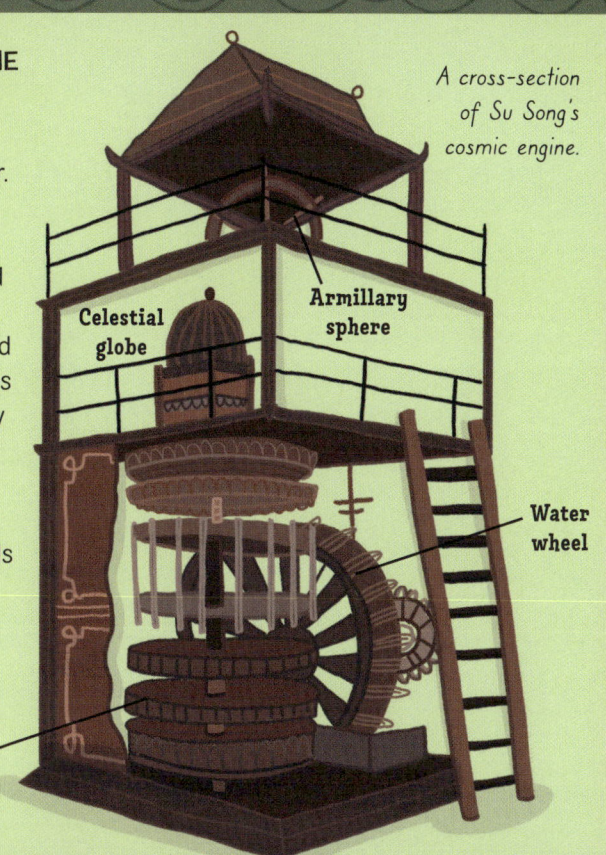

A cross-section of Su Song's cosmic engine.

Celestial globe · Armillary sphere · Water wheel · Clockwork mechanism

Festivals

Chinese New Year was (and is) a huge festival. Celebrations to greet it carried on for 15 days, ending with the Lantern Festival at the first full moon of the year.

At the Lantern Festival, Ah Lam and other children carry lanterns through the streets alongside a parade of dancing dragons.

Our dragon will scare away evil...

Good luck with the New Year!

Look at my lantern!

THE ALCHEMIST'S CHILDREN

From the earliest times, the Chinese were great inventors. Some of their breakthroughs came from alchemy, a sort of early science that in China was particularly linked to medicine. Alchemists looked for elixirs – potions that would make you live forever. They never found one but they made plenty of other discoveries!

Hello, I'm Tao. I'm studying to be an alchemist, just like my dad.

Hello, I'm Yu Yan. I'm Tao's sister, I'd like to be an alchemist, too, even though I'm a girl.

TAO

YU YAN

Look out!

That was a surprise!

Let's do that again!

A serious science
These days alchemy is often linked with magic but back then it was not seen that way. It was strongly linked with the beliefs of Taoism (see page 39) and it was taken very seriously.

Women alchemists
Whilst most alchemists were men, there were a few well-known women alchemists. For example, Keng Hsien-Seng, who lived in the 10th century, was admired for her use of mercury to extract silver from its ore.

How gunpowder was invented
Today Tao, his dad and Yu Yan are experimenting with heating three materials to make an elixir: saltpetre (potassium nitrate), wood charcoal (carbon) and sulphur. Suddenly there is a huge bang and the pan explodes! This probably describes how a Chinese alchemist discovered gunpowder. No one knows exactly when but gunpowder was in use by the 9th century.

Rockets developed as weapons from fire arrows. They could set fire to buildings during a siege.

Use of gunpowder
The Chinese first used fireworks for lighting up the sky at New Year celebrations. But weapons soon followed (see page 21), including rockets and canons. The use of gunpowder spread to Asia and Europe in the 13th century, perhaps along the Silk Road, changing the way people waged war forever.

CHINA'S MANY INVENTIONS

China is credited with many 'firsts' in technological history. Some of these were then copied elsewhere in the world, others were just invented separately. Here is a 'Top 15' with links to other pages in this book.

LIST OF TOP 15 INVENTIONS

The first four are often called China's 'Four Great Inventions'.
1. Paper - see page 24
2. Printing - see page 25
3. Gunpowder - see opposite and page 21
4. The compass
5. Silk - see page 22
6. The wheelbarrow - see page 12
7. Clockwork - see page 27
8. The paddy field - see page 13
9. Parasol
10. Porcelain
11. Kite
12. Tea
13. Seed drill
14. Smelting iron
15. Seismometer (earthquake detector)

Parasol
The parasol or umbrella gave protection from both the sun and the rain. Its ribbed structure was already in use by the Qin dynasty.

Seed drill
A seed drill plants seeds at a regular depth in the soil. An ox-pulled version was invented by a scholar-official during the Han dynasty.

Tea
The Chinese started using tea leaves for medicinal drinks over 4,000 years ago. The tea plant is native to China.

Compass
The first Chinese compasses were used by the Han dynasty to check that buildings were in harmony and balance with their surroundings. They used a lodestone (a natural magnet) which made a bowl with a pointer spin and show the direction of south. This idea was later adapted for navigation.

Kites
Using a bamboo frame, silk and later paper were ideal for making kites. Legend dates their invention to the 5th century BCE.

Hand-operated bellows

Smelting iron
The Chinese developed ways of smelting iron, extracting it from its ore, at very high temperatures, using bellows to blow air on the furnace. The iron became liquid and could be poured into moulds to shape.

Earthquake detector
Zhang Heng (see page 31) created this device. Delicately balanced inside it were balls that dropped from a dragon's mouth into a toad's when there was an earthquake. It showed in which direction the earthquake was happening, as far away as 500 km.

Porcelain
The Chinese began to develop the techniques of making this fine, semi-transparent ceramic during the Han dynasty. It was highly-prized around the world.

FAMOUS CHINESE DOCTORS

The traditions of Chinese medicine date back a long time and some of its earliest famous doctors are part of legend, rather than historic fact. There are many later famous doctors, too.

Shennong is a legendary ruler known as the Father of Chinese Medicine. He is said to be the author of one of the first books on Chinese traditional medicine.

Huangdi (the Yellow Emperor) is another legendary ruler. He is credited with developing acupuncture.

Tan Yunxian (1461–1554 CE) learnt medicine from her grandparents. As was usual at that time for female doctors, she only treated women.

THE TRAINEE DOCTOR

A doctor in ancient China was trained by helping an older, more experienced doctor. They learnt practical skills, like making medicine or surgery, but also the complicated ideas and beliefs behind health. Young doctors like Qin soon discovered it was all about balance.

Hello, I'm Qin. I'm learning to be a doctor. Hua is teaching me. He knows a lot!

HUA
QIN

I gather herbs to bring you long life.

Yin and Yang were part of Chinese Taoist beliefs. Magu is their goddess of long life, linked to traditional medicine.

Traditional Chinese medicine
The Chinese believed that there were two opposing forces in the universe, Yin (passive) and Yang (active), This included in the human body. People became ill when these forces were out of balance. A doctor's job was to correct this, often with medicines. These were made from a large range of natural materials, from dried plants to animal parts.

Qi and acupuncture
Doctors also had to understand *qi* – people's life force which flowed through the body in invisible channels called meridians. Problems with the flow of *qi* could cause ill health and pain. During the Han era, doctors developed acupuncture to treat this. Very thin needles were inserted at points on the meridians. The needles stimulated the flow of *qi* and corrected the Yin and Yang balance.

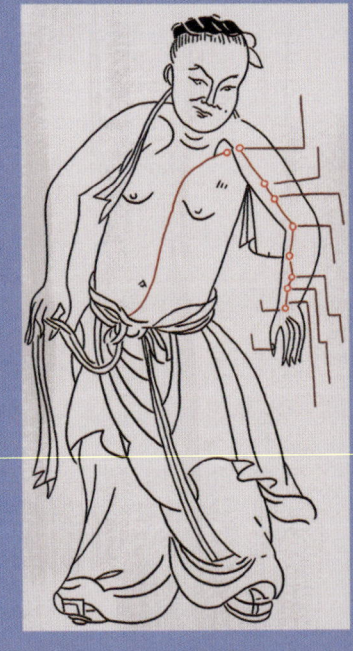

Qin will learn the pressure points on the meridians. This picture shows those on the arm and shoulder.

Surgery

Doctors only operated on people if it was absolutely necessary. Hua Tuo (c. 140–208 CE), an expert doctor who is sometimes called the Father of Chinese Surgery, performed many operations successfully, including on the stomach. He took out parts of the intestine, washed them and stitched them back in place.

Sleeping drugs

Hua Tuo also developed the first anaesthetics. He put his patients to sleep with powerful opium-based herbs mixed in wine. Records say a patient was pain free after five days and better after a month. Hua Tuo also recommended exercise as part of a patient's recovery.

I make a small incision here. Pass the swab, please!

Coming right up.

Zzzzzzzz.

Hua is an expert surgeon. Qin is happy to be able to assist him.

SCIENCE IN ANCIENT CHINA

As well as great advances in technology, the Chinese also made many scientific discoveries and developed advanced mathematics.

A Chinese abacus was called a 'saunpan', which means calculating tray.

An armillary sphere was made of interlocking rings linked to the stars and planets. At their centre was the Earth. The flow of water made these rings slowly rotate, moving the objects at the same speed as they moved in the sky.

Using an abacus

The Chinese developed an abacus for counting and calculation. It was used for everything, from keeping accounts to exploring the night sky. Maths was a general part of a boy's education and there were many high-flying mathematicians among the scholar-officials.

Studying the stars

Astronomy was also an important area of study, partly because it was associated with timekeeping (see page 27). The Han dynasty astronomer and inventor Zhang Heng (78–139 CE) mapped over 2,500 stars and 100 constellations. Around 125 CE, he developed a water-powered armillary sphere. It showed the movements of the sun, moon and stars.

GREAT POETS

Here are just a few of China's many famous poets.

Li Bai (701–762 CE) was a Tang dynasty poet admired for his poems celebrating friendship, solitude and drinking.

Du Fu (712–770 CE) was a Tang politician. He is known for his powerful poetry about the effects of war.

Li Qingzhao (1084–1155 CE) wrote during the Song dynasty. The daughter of poets, she started young. She wrote movingly about love, and later war. Today she is one of China's most famous poets.

THE YOUNG POET

Writing developed very early in China and with it a rich tradition of poetry and other literature. Not many Chinese women received a formal education, but a few did, the number growing over the centuries. Some became known for their beautiful poetry.

Writing poetry
Most educated Chinese wrote poetry, often linked to nature. They were taught how to structure their poems in a particular way. Some forms dated back thousands of years. During the Tang and Song dynasties, poetry flourished among the scholar-official class. New free and expressive forms of poetry developed.

The literary life
The Chinese held poetry parties. Friends met to talk and exchange ideas. They drank rice wine and played games, which often included reciting or even composing poems. Baozhai is at a 'Winding Stream Party' and it is her turn.

Hello, I'm Baozhai. I'm 15 and love to write poetry. I use my best calligraphy so it looks good, too.

BAOZHAI

Cups of wine were dropped in the water. If a cup stopped before you, you had to make up a poem on the spot – or drink the wine.

The cup has stopped by Baozhai!

I always remember the sunset by the river...

Come on! Let's hear your poem

A winding stream party often used specially-built channels.

Origins of writing in China

The Chinese began to use a form of writing around 4,000 years ago. They carved pictograms onto bones and tortoise shells. These developed into characters. Each character represents a word or part of a word, which are then combined to make another word. Today there are over 50,000 characters but only about 16 per cent of these are used regularly.

The carved pictograms of early Chinese were used to predict the future. These 'oracle bones', like this piece of tortoise shell, linked to early beliefs in magic.

Developing characters

Various different character systems developed in the different regions of China. These were standardised during the Qin dynasty, bringing together the newly united country under one system. The shape and form of characters developed over time too.

The early pictograms developed into more stylised shapes that were quicker to write and carve. The fourth column shows traditional characters. These were simplified still further in 1949.

God of writing

The ancient Chinese asked the god of writing, Wenchang Wang, for inspiration. Students today call on him for help with exams.

Wenchang Wang travels with two servants behind him, described as 'Deaf as Heaven' and 'Mute as Earth'.

The written word

The Chinese did not just write about poetry, they wrote about everything: history, science, religion, philosophy and many 'how to' manuals. People collected and told traditional stories and legends. In the Ming dynasty, novels became popular.

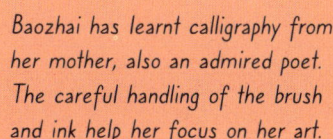

Sima Qian (c .145–86 BCE) wrote one of the first histories of ancient China.

Calligraphy

Perhaps because of their pictogram origins, the Chinese soon elevated writing into the art of calligraphy. Characters were painted with soft, animal-hair brushes. Focusing on what you were doing and following the movement of the brush was considered just as creative as what you were writing, and the two were completely tied together.

Baozhai has learnt calligraphy from her mother, also an admired poet. The careful handling of the brush and ink help her focus on her art.

"Calligraphy puts me in the creative zone!"

THE PEAR GARDEN

Hello! I'm Feiyan. I'm a student at the Pear Garden Academy.

FEIYAN

Feiyan is a talented musician. She plays the pipa, a kind of lute with strings that are plucked.

The arts – including poetry, music, dance and painting – were always popular in ancient China. During the Tang dynasty (618–907), the Emperor Xuanzong made many reforms to how the country was run. It led to a Golden Age of peace and prosperity. Xuanzong built roads and temples. He also built the Pear Garden Academy, a school for music and performing arts.

Wu is playing the konghou, a kind of harp.

Hou plucks the strings of a ruan.

Yongtai is playing a kind of flute called a hulusi.

Yang plays a dizi, a type of flute.

The guzheng was a large stringed instrument similar to a zither.

Feiyan and her group will play at the banquet.

Music
In China, the first flutes date to 8,000 years ago, and the first orchestras to 3,000 years ago. By the Tang dynasty, the Chinese had developed a system of notation, to write down the music they played.

The twins are wearing traditional Tang dynasty dance costumes. The sleeves of their dresses are much longer than their arms.

Dance
Dancing reached a peak during the Tang dynasty. Many new dances were invented and recorded. Some of the best-known dances, such as the Lion Dance, date to this time.

Greetings! We are twin sisters, Mu-lan and Mu-lin. We will do the Blessed Goddess Dance at the banquet.

MU-LAN   MU-LIN

We have a state banquet next week. The students will entertain important guests.

Hiya! I'm Feng. We're rehearsing our act for the Emperor's banquet. He's come to watch.

Feng's group perform acrobatic gymnastics, doing somersaults, jumps, kicks and balancing acts that require strength and coordination.

XUANZONG

FENG

The Pear Garden Academy
About 300 young musicians and performers studied every year at the Pear Garden. The Emperor took a close interest in the school. The students performed at state banquets and official ceremonies.

Acrobatics
Acrobatic acts date to the origins of Chinese history. They mingled with folk dances and were performed by working people. During the Tang dynasty they became more artistic – a bit like ballet.

Masks
Performers wear make-up or masks with strong colours. The colours have meanings: a green mask symbolises brutality and bravery, while red means courage and loyalty. Blue means stubborness.

CHINESE OPERA
Chinese opera is a kind of musical theatre that developed gradually over hundreds of years. It combines the music, dance and acrobatics of earlier performances, and reached its maturity during the Song dynasty (960—1279). It continued to develop and is still enjoyed today. There are many different forms all over China.

Opera dancers use hand gestures to convey additional messages.

Sword fight   **Indicating ones head or heaven**   **Holding a fan upside down**   **A fist for a fight or battle**

The Monkey King is a famous piece in the Beijing Opera today. It is based on a classic Chinese novel from the Ming era.

GOODS TO TRADE

Silk was not the only thing sold along the Silk Road. Legend has it that the Chinese originally went to Central Asia to buy 'heavenly horses'. The Chinese traded their goods (silk, porcelain, paper, tea) for things they wanted (cotton cloth, woollen rugs, gems and glass). Food and spices were traded in both directions.

BANDITS ON THE SILK ROAD

The traders on the Silk Road did not travel all the way from China to the Mediterranean Sea. The road was more a network of many routes linking different places. A merchant would take his goods some of the way to sell them in the markets of the cities that grew up along the routes. The journeys were still long and dangerous, crossing deserts and high mountains. Bandits would hide in these lonely places, hoping for an opportunity to attack.

A trading caravan

Bigan and his dad set out in a small caravan, just a couple of camels and a horse. The animals are laden with goods. Bigan's dad is hopeful he will get a better price if he travels as far as Kashgar. It is worth the risk.

Small caravans often travelled the Silk Road but they also grouped together for safety. They stopped at inns called caravanserais each night.

ANCIENT BELIEFS

Some of the influences on Chinese religion are very ancient, probably going back to the first farmers. People believed in spirits that controlled the earth and lived in nature. People made offerings to the spirits to ensure good harvests.

There were good and evil spirits. The good fought against the evil. This cast-iron face is a Toatie, one of the evil spirits. It was made over 3,000 years ago.

Ancestor worship

The ancient Chinese celebrated their ancestors. They were part of their ancient beliefs in the spirit world that surrounds us all the time. Ancestors were treated as minor gods and remembered through many rituals. Ancestor worship continues to this day, often as part of the other religions.

The Chinese often set up shrines to their ancestors in their homes.

THE YOUNG MONK

It was not just goods that were exchanged along the Silk and Spice routes – so were ideas and beliefs. One of the most important of these was Buddhism. Monks brought this religion to China along the trade routes during the Han dynasty. About 600 years later, a Chinese monk decided to travel back to India, where Buddhism came from.

Hello, I'm Li Sou. I'm 15 and a novice – a trainee Buddhist monk. I'm off to India.

LI SOU

Li Sou entered a Buddhist monastery at 13 as a novice, when his head was shaved. He should become a monk around the age of 20, but his travels might delay that..

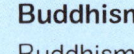

The more you give, the more comes to you.

Buddhism

Buddhism was founded in India by Siddhartha Gautama, known as the Buddha, who lived around the 6th century BCE. Buddhists believe that, after we die, we are reborn in another life. The Buddha taught people to break out of this cycle of life and death through thinking deeply and living a good life. In China, as in other countries, Buddhism took on elements of existing beliefs. This helped it to mix with, and greatly influence, China's culture.

The Laughing Buddha, or Budai, was a 10th-century Chinese monk known for his cheerful nature. His round figure has become a popular symbol of happiness.

The Yuantong Buddhist Temple or 'Temple of the comprehension of all things' dates from the Tang dynasty. It shows the unique Chinese style for Buddhist temples and monasteries.

Xuanzang

The Chinese Buddhist monk Xuanzang (602–664) travelled through China looking for sacred Buddhist texts, but he became concerned that those China had were incomplete and poorly translated. He decided to make a pilgrimage to India in search of the originals.

--- Xuanzang's journey

Xuanzang travelled to India alone but he might have taken a novice like Li Sou with him. Li Sou would learn from Xuanzang on the way.

I wish to go and find out the truth.

On his return to China, Xuanzang lived in a Buddhist monastery and told his fellow monks about his travels. Three of them wrote down his adventures in a famous travelogue.

A 16-year pilgrimage

Xuanzang travelled the Silk Road to Central Asia and then south to India. He travelled all over the country talking to other Buddhists and collecting sacred texts. Often on foot, he travelled over 16,000 km. He returned to China with 657 texts. He spent much of the rest of his life translating the most important of these into Chinese.

But it's a very long walk to India...

Xuanzang's travels inspired a famous 16th century Chinese novel called **Journey to the West**. In this story, Xuanzang had three companions, including the Monkey King (see page 35).

Never impose on others what you would not choose for yourself.

Knowing others is intelligence; knowing yourself is true wisdom.

CONFUCIANISM

Confucius (551–479 BCE) was one of the most influential Chinese thinkers that ever lived. He believed you should treat everyone justly, with respect and kindness, whether inside the family or a public organisation. Confucianism was more moral guidance on how to lead your life rather than a religion. It had no gods or belief in an afterlife. This meant other religions could work within it. It also gave a useful framework for running the huge Chinese Empire.

The Chinese character for water is a symbol for Confucianism. Water is a source of life.

Confucius was both a philosopher and a politician. He believed it was important to study to rule well.

TAOISM (OR DAOISM)

This Chinese religion developed from the teachings of Laozi, a philosopher who lived around the same time as Confucius. Laozi encouraged people to be spiritual and to follow the 'Way' (*Tao*). This involved being close to nature, thinking deeply and living in harmony with the world. This harmony was maintained when the two opposing forces in the universe, the Yin (passive) and Yang (active), were in balance. Like other Chinese faiths, Taoism worked easily with other beliefs and religious practices.

In legend, after writing down his ideas, Laozi was last seen riding a water buffalo over the Chinese border.

The Yin and Yang symbol is older than Taoism but is often used to represent the religion.

THE MATCHMAKER'SASSISTANT

Confucius thought the family was at the heart of Chinese life. Marriage built families so it was equally important. The Chinese married not for love but to make the family strong. A matchmaker often helped them find the right person for this.

Hello, I'm Li. I'm 17 and help Zhang. I let her know about people looking to get married.

I'm old Zhang! I'm a matchmaker. Everyone knows me. I need undercover help to do my job.

Making a choice
Chinese usually married people from the same background as themselves. By law, they had to marry someone with a different surname. A matchmaker like Zhang looked for possible partners who brought benefits to the family. She helped arrange an exchange of gifts between the two families – there was a lot of haggling.

Li helps the bride put on her make-up on the day of the wedding and does her hair so she looks beautiful. She follows traditional styles.

The Tea Ceremony
A couple were officially engaged after suitable gifts were agreed. The wedding took place inside the bride's home in front of the family shrine. From at least the Tang dynasty onwards, a tea ceremony followed, where bride and groom served tea to their new families.

The bride goes first. Make your bow...

Please have a cup of tea, Po Po.

You have a good bride, my son.

The couple use formal terms to address their family at the ceremony. A mother-in-law is 'po po', a father-in-law 'gong gong'.

Zhang has done her job well.

The tea ceremony allows the bride and groom to greet their new families formally and to show their respect. Li guides them.

A Chinese childhood

Whilst wealthy boys went to school, most children stayed at home and learnt from their parents. They helped out on the farm or in the family workshop. Girls learnt about keeping house from their mothers. All children were taught to respect their parents.

Look! I can do a keepie uppie.

Fun and games

Children might work hard and have to do what they were told, but they had time for fun and games. It was important to have lots of children that were healthy and happy to ensure the family continued. Many Chinese paintings featured children at play. Pictures like these symbolised success and prosperity within the family.

Ball games were popular with both boys and girls. 'Cuju' was a bit like football and considered a good form of exercise.

Slides were fun. Wealthy families built them in their gardens.

Wheee…

Yikes! I can't stop.

You win again!

Children learnt how to play boardgames. The game 'Go' is around 4,000 years old. It remains popular today.

HOMES AND HOUSES

After marriage, a bride moved into her husband's family home. All the generations of a family lived together in one house: children, parents, grandparents and more. The new bride worked alongside the other women of the house to look after it and the men. Traditionally, men came first in every household, rich or poor. Houses were also built following traditional styles and rules.

A COURTYARD HOUSE OR 'SIHEYUAN'

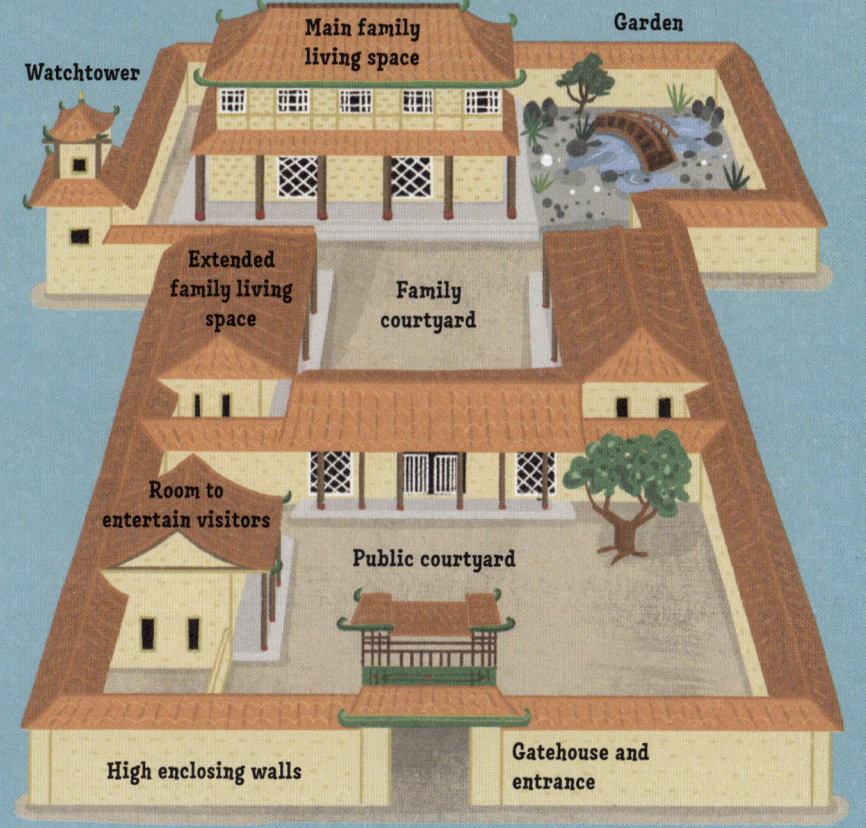

Poor families lived in one-roomed houses. Doors and windows faced south to ensure a house was in harmony with its surroundings.

Richer families had larger homes with one or more courtyards. These houses also faced south. There was space for a large family and their servants.

QUIZ TIME!

Let's check and see how much you learned! Don't worry if you don't know all the answers. You can look back through the pages and find them. The answers to the quiz are on page 44, just below the Index.

1. Ancient China was first united as an empire over 2,000 years ago by Qin Shi Huang.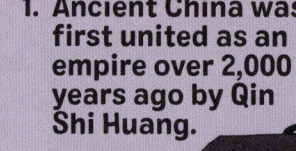
   ○ TRUE
   ○ FALSE

2. Which of these are true about Chinese rice farming?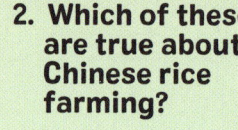
   A. They used paddy fields
   B. They used ploughs
   C. They planted by hand
   D. It was their only crop

3. Chinese emperors were religious leaders. What did they have to do?
   A. Study hard
   B. Make sacrifices
   C. Say prayers
   D. Be called 'the Son of Heaven'
   E. All of the above

4. There was never a female emperor of China.
   ○ TRUE   ○ FALSE

5. To become a member of the Chinese civil service you had to:
   A. Learn to write
   B. Pass exams
   C. Be a poet
   D. Study the writings of Confucius

6. Which of these statements are true about the Great Wall of China?
   A. No one ever broke through it
   B. It is over 20,000 km long
   C. Six horses could ride side-by-side along it
   D. Soldiers lit beacons to send messages along it

7. Silkworms are the caterpillars of butterflies.
   ○ TRUE
   ○ FALSE

8. The first dynasty to issue official banknotes was the Song.
   ○ TRUE
   ○ FALSE

9. When is the Chinese Lantern Festival?
   A. Midsummer
   B. In the autumn
   C. The start of the Chinese New Year
   D. 15 days after the start of the Chinese New Year

10. Gunpowder was invented by mistake.
    ○ TRUE   ○ FALSE

11. Which of these were invented by the Chinese?

A. The compass
B. The wheelbarrow
C. Paper
D. Printing
E. All of the above

12. What is the name of the water-powered machine made by Zhang Heng to study the movement of the stars?

A. A compass
B. A telescope
C. A globe
D. An armillary sphere

13. Which of these is the name for a Chinese poetry party game?

A. Poetry Please
B. Winding Stream
C. Poetry Jam
D. Your Turn Next
E. Make It Rhyme

14. Performers wear masks in Chinese opera.

○ TRUE ○ FALSE

15. There was a school for performing arts during the Tang dynasty called the Apple Garden.

○ TRUE ○ FALSE

16. The Spice Routes were a network of sea trade routes linking China with Europe.

○ TRUE ○ FALSE

17. Which of these statements are NOT true of the Silk Road?

A. It was an overland trade route
B. Paper was one of the goods traded along it
C. It went round the Taklamakan Desert
D. The groups of camels and traders that travelled on it were called lorries

18. Which of these religions was not widely practised in ancient China?

A. Buddhism
B. Hinduism
C. Confucianism
D. Taoism
E. Ancestor worship

19. When does the Chinese Tea Ceremony take place?

A. At a birthday party
B. At an engagement party
C. At a naming ceremony
D. After a wedding ceremony

20. A large courtyard house was called a 'siheyuan'.

○ TRUE ○ FALSE

INDEX

A
Acrobatics 35
Alchemy 28
Ancestors 38
Animals 12, 26, 36
Astronomy 27, 31

B
Buddhism 10, 38-39

C
Calendars 26
Calligraphy 18, 32, 33
Childhood 41
Civil service 10, 18-19, 26
Clocks 26-27
Clothes 16, 23
Concubines 14, 16-17, 19
Confucius 10, 18, 19, 39, 40

D
Dance 34-35
Doctors 16, 30-31
Dynasties 10, 14, 15

E
Emperor 10, 14-15, 16-17, 18, 19, 20, 21, 22, 23, 30, 34, 35
Empress 16-17, 23
Exams 18-19, 33

F
Family 12, 14-15, 16, 18, 19, 39, 40-41
Farming 12-13, 18, 41
Festivals 27

G
Great Wall 10, 12, 15, 20-21
Gunpowder 21, 28, 29

H
Homes 19, 38, 41

I
Inventions 10, 12, 21, 23, 28, 29

M
Magic 28, 33
Marriage 16, 40-41
Medicine 24, 28, 30
Money 18, 22, 25
Mongols 10, 21
Monks 38-39
Music 18, 34-35

N
Navy 20

O
Opera 35

P
Palaces 10, 15, 16-17
Paper 23, 24-25, 29, 36
Poetry 18, 19, 32-33, 34
Printing 25, 29

R
Rice 12-13

S
Scholar-officials 18-19, 27, 29, 31, 32
Schools 10, 18, 34, 35, 41
Science 28, 31, 33
Silk 22-23, 29, 36
Silk Road 10, 22, 28, 36-37, 38, 39
Soldiers 20-21
Spice Routes 37, 38
Surgery 31

T
Taoism 28, 39
Tea 13, 14, 23, 24, 29, 36, 40
Temples 15, 34, 38
Time 26-27, 31
Trade 10, 19, 20, 22, 36-37, 38

W
Weapons 21, 28
Women 16-17, 22, 28, 32, 41
Writing 10, 18, 19, 24, 25, 32-33

ANSWERS TO THE QUIZ
(pages 42-43)

1	True	8	True	15	False
2	A, B, C	9	D	16	True
3	E	10	True	17	D
4	False	11	E	18	B
5	A, B, D	12	D	19	D
6	B, D	13	B	20	True
7	False	14	True